T0128648

Smorgasbord of Poetry

AuthorHouse™
1663 Liberty Drive
Bloomington, IN 47403
www.authorhouse.com
Phone: 833-262-8899

This book is printed on acid-free paper.

ISBN: 978-1-6655-2541-1 (sc)
ISBN: 978-1-6655-2542-8 (e)

Print information available on the last page.

Published by AuthorHouse 05/10/2021

authorHOUSE

Smorgasbord of Poetry

A collection of Love, Satirical and Haiku poems

By Danen J. Wilson

Shadows of the Heart

As night draws near, my love comes here

So as the heart shiver's through fear

As When two hearts shines like a beaming light,

So as shadows reflect through the light.

As night comes nigh and the day passes by.

So as two hearts beats like a dancing drum,

When two people Dance through the calming night

So as love comes hither

When love flys like the dazzling kite

So as blood reflect like shallowly blithe

As shadows reflects from the beaming light

Here comes love blowing like the misty night.

Day # Two Haiku Poem -Mystery

An untold fact:

Draws a person to react,

So is a Mystery to those who knows the facts.

Day # Three Satire Poem

As a lazy bird who doesn't surge

So as a lazy person who lacks the urge.

When time draw near who crys come here

So as a lazy ear whose screams I can't hear.

When hearing crys to the simple peer,

Who is that person whose runs to hear?

Day # four Deceit

Like a magician trick in disguised,

So as truth, hidden in a lie.

As a person reveals more lies, and lots of untruth

So as honesty is meant to reveal the truth.

After chance, after chance to reveal the truth,

As person continue to hide in disguised to reveal their truth.

Day # Five Treachery Haiku Poem

The allegiance of faith is bound up like a broken glass,

So as treason overshadows the ties of reason that never passes.

Sands of Love

As one walks along the sandy beach,

Glancing and prancing through the summer heat,

Just like a feather that breaks from heat.

As wave and current beats along the brink,

So as sands of love comes from beneath.

As hearts and kisses from lovers that meet,

That reaches the hearts of those who preach.

So as sands of love from the beach.

Trees of Light

As Birds sings and swans swim,

So as leaves begins to grimm,

As hearts shines and laughter brings joy,

So as lights begins to shine of joy.

As fruit blossoms and spring blooms,

So as that great tree that brings light

Hikers Bliss

As one who seeks to explore the horizon,

So as a hiker gets an arisen,

As trails becomes like a blistering stone,

So as the feet of the hiker begins to plum.

Step by step, hip by hip, So as the hiker begins to take a dip.

Around the way, around the pond, each hiker travels far home.

Lovers Thirst

As water quenches a thirsty soul,

So as love quenches as deprive soul,

As happiness bubbles like a sparkling drink,

So as love heals that parch beak,

As times heals and wounds turn from dill,

So will love fills that thirsty heel.

Trouble ♥

The hourly glass that drips the sand,

So as the heart begins to band.

As beats tremble and the heart that scribbles

So as the person who heart is troubled.

As the waves beat upon the bank,

So as problems comes like a tank.

To the one who has a trouble heart there is comfort in those that shows love.

Printed in the United States
by Baker & Taylor Publisher Services